Yes Virginia,
There is a
Cure for Diabetes

Yes Virginia, There is a Cure for Diabetes

HAL CHRISTENSEN

authorHOUSE®

AuthorHouse™
1663 Liberty Drive
Bloomington, IN 47403
www.authorhouse.com
Phone: 1 (800) 839-8640

Published by AuthorHouse   08/05/2015

ISBN: 978-1-4817-1769-4 (sc)
ISBN: 978-1-4817-2987-1 (e)

Library of Congress Control Number: 2013905019

Print information available on the last page.

This book is printed on acid-free paper.

I dedicate this book to the two most influential women in my life. First to my mother, Virginia, for giving every moment of her life to being a better mother for her children and for instilling happiness in my life.

And to Katie, my beautiful wife and best friend, who has always loved me unconditionally and tries every day to teach me patience.

INTRODUCTION

I began this autobiography about ten years ago, and my attention to it has come and gone. I hope that it will be of interest to many and a help for others. The title of this story refers to juvenile, or type 1 diabetes. It's a significant portion of my life I write about, from age ten to age forty. It is the true account of how I acquired juvenile diabetes at an early age and fought its deadly effects for thirty years. Somehow I was blessed beyond blessed to have this cure, this miracle come into my life and make me a person of normal health again. I am sure there are those who will disagree with me that an organ transplant isn't a real cure for juvenile diabetes. I counter that argument with, "Just what does a cure have to consist of?" From my viewpoint, my cure has taken all the terrible aspects of diabetes out of my life, never to return, unless I were to just give up on taking care of myself. If all I have to do is monitor my health, which everyone should do anyway, and take two pills twice a day, that is a pretty good trade-off, I think.

What inspired me to finish my story this time was a nurse in a hospital. I was in for an intestinal obstruction due to some scar tissue from the transplant, and I related a bit of my story to her. She said that I should write it down, because, she said, "You don't hear stories like that much." What I know for certain is that without this miracle cure, I would not be here today.

CHAPTER 1

Juvenile Diabetes, the Beginning

As the cool song lyrics by Bryan Adams goes, "It was the summer of 69," but I wasn't cool, I was just your average ten-year-old kid, and being cool wouldn't be important for a few more years. My family and I were on our way to attend the grand McEntire Family Reunion, held every year in Preston, Idaho. This trip from my hometown of Twin Falls, Idaho, always took us about four hours. Dad was adamantly against taking any shortcuts to make this trip quicker. As I grew older and took my own family to the reunion, the trip unaccountably shortened to about three hours—but I guess speed limits have changed too!

This quiet little town of Preston was the birthplace of my mother, Virginia McEntire Christensen. My dad was born and raised just down the road and over the state border, fourteen miles away in an even smaller Utah town called Richmond. The McEntire reunions were a much anticipated event each year and are still held today, although the numbers are dwindling as the original siblings continue to pass away. Mom came from a family of nine children, so there were many relations in attendance, including lots of cousins to play with. These were great times to be had for a kid like me. "City kids" we were labeled, even though my so-called city had a population of only twenty-one thousand residents. We were so named because of the fact that we lived in towns and not on farms. Two of my uncles owned dairy farms in Preston, and at least to me, that was city kid heaven! But this was also where I remember my beginnings with the dreaded disease, juvenile diabetes.

Before continuing with that portion of my story, I should tell what brought me to that part of my life. I believe I had the best childhood a kid could ever want. I had my free agency, or so I always thought, to do whatever I wanted and to explore wherever I wished. Mom sure kept a close watch on me though. One of my earliest memories is of my first trip to test my independence. I was only five or six years old, and Mom allowed me to take lunch trips, which I called camping trips, but they were just to the edge of the front lawn! Mom would pack me a small lunch, tie it up in one of Dad's bandanna handkerchiefs, and then tie that to an old stick, and off I would go by myself on a glorious adventure— all that way! I don't know why, but I had a fascination with the life of a Hobo, and many of my Halloween costumes turned out to be Hobo themed; but us kids just got a kick out of calling them Bums!

I grew up a fairly happy kid. I know now that my parents didn't make a lot of money, but I never lacked for anything. They always tried to make life happy and enjoyable. I will relate more of that later on.

CHAPTER 2

The Grand Family Reunion

Back to the big McEntire reunion, my favorite times away from home. Some of the things I did may have been the catalyst for my diabetes rolling forward. Even though juvenile, or type 1 diabetes is predominantly of a hereditary nature, I feel sure that a person can speed up its onset by overindulgence, and I certainly did plenty of that! Sugar and goodies were my pals, and I could not get enough of them.

My cousin Jon who lived on the dairy farm was, shall we say, oh just a bit spoiled. Where I mostly got bland cereals like Cheerios and Corn Flakes for breakfast at my house, my aunt Jan's pantry was stocked with every conceivable sugar-coated cereal on the market. It was breakfast heaven for me, and I had to try them all. Then there was the milk. Remember this was a dairy farm and there wasn't any skim, 2% or even whole milk that was bought from a store. This was "fresh from the cow with all the cream you can stand" milk, and it was so good!

Jon and I would sometimes grab an empty pitcher, two large glasses, and a container of chocolate drink mix from the kitchen and head for the barn where the big five-hundred-gallon holding tank was; this tank was the first destination for the milk as it came from the cow. Now we didn't get our milk from the spout at the bottom of the tank to make our batch of chocolate milk, oh no we scooped it right off the top, you know where all the cream rises to! Now that was some very good, very rich chocolate milk, a heart attack in the planning for sure.

To describe the reunion food, it certainly had nothing to do with calorie counting, or weight control, but quite the opposite. Reunion time was the time for indulgence in every sense of the word. I always enjoyed watching my uncle Reed make the Dutch Oven potatoes or funeral potatoes, as they were appropriately named in this part of the country. Not only because you would eventually die from eating them, but because, as members of the Mormon Church, we made them for every funeral dinner! My uncle's recipe was slightly altered you could say. He started with the biggest Dutch oven available and filled it with sliced potatoes. Then he would add one pound of butter chunked up, a big cup of onions, and the icing on this widow-maker was a full pound of sliced cheese on top! Oh man, when you ate these, you could *feel* yourself getting fatter! My grandparents held a long tradition of serving fried chicken, and they loved it, so there was always lots of it at our reunions. To top off this lavish feast, everyone brought multiple salads and desserts. If possible, home-made ice cream was also served.

A good point to make here is that of these senior McEntire siblings, most have lived into their nineties, and of those that have died, I don't believe any of them died from heart attacks or heart disease. I stand convinced that a legacy of a strong Scottish "McEntire" heart beats in our bodies, and the family has a good health history to prove it. A history of diabetes also is present because my grandpa had it, but I was the only child that got juvenile diabetes. There were several family members including my mother, who acquired adult onset diabetes as they aged.

So I was busy playing at the reunion as always this particular summer, but in the midst of all this childhood frolicking, I began to notice that for some reason my mom was concerned about all the water I was drinking. I figured that because it was hot and I was running around a lot, I was just thirstier. She also kept an eye on my bathroom trips, which became very frequent. As alarmed as a ten year old could get with all of the great attractions to participate in, I mustered as much concern as I could. I thought to myself, "There must be something wrong with me, but I'm sure I don't know what it could be," so I dismissed it and went on enjoying life.

CHAPTER 3

School Begins, Diabetes Looms

Things with my health must have calmed down after the reunion, or else my mom just couldn't face the fact that something was wrong with her baby. You see, the reunion was usually held in late July, and I recall that when I was diagnosed with juvenile diabetes, I had to be taken out of school, and was in the hospital for ten days to get regulated. So the onset must have happened a couple of months later. During my hospital stay, I lost over ten pounds! How my mom knew the warning signs of diabetes back then I'm not sure, but you can bet that as a ten year old kid, I didn't know what was wrong with me.

After the diagnosis, old Dr. Schow immediately admitted me to the hospital. My condition had been explained to me, but all I remembered were two things, I could no longer have *any* sugar, and I had to take shots, (injections of insulin) every day—*yikes*! Shots and I went way back. I hated them, because every time I got sick Mom hauled me off to Dr. Schow for a big penicillin shot. He would pull out a needle so long I swear it had to bypass my arm bone to go all the way in! When he hit me with that spike, it felt as if he just made a big fist and punched me as hard as he could! In those days they didn't use disposable needles; they just soaked them in alcohol and reused them. I'm sure I always got the dull ones just before they were sent out for resharpening! My only reward or bribe for that shot was getting a big ice cream cone afterward; of course, that was before diabetes.

So my life as a diabetic had begun. I returned to school after those ten days, and oddly enough I was something of a celebrity among my school chums. They all huddled around me like I had won a big prize or something. They wanted to know what exactly I had because back then, diabetes was somewhat of a mystery disease. I certainly don't want it back, but today the way they advertise it and all the great products for taking care of it, they make people who have it seem like celebrities. It's almost cool to have diabetes—*not*!

Adjustments to my lifestyle had to be made, and over the next few months, my sugar levels bounced up and down a lot. Checking blood sugar level was quite primitive in 1969 with only urine dip sticks available. I had to pee in a cup, then dip the test strip in and wait one minute. I also had ketone testing strips, this was the big "no no never go there" test. If your blood sugar ever got high enough to register ketoacidosis, you were in serious trouble! These tests weren't too accurate and have been replaced with blood glucose testing. This testing method has now prevented the majority of episodes where ketoacidosis, or very high blood sugar can occur, because the testing is almost instantaneous.

Chapter 4

Growing Up with Diabetes

As I grew into adolescence, my body was plagued with many new experiences with diabetes. Most memorable was the low blood sugar. Not eating enough or taking too much insulin caused this. I would start to feel all weak and begin to shake. If that went on long enough, my thoughts became scrambled.

I remember only one really bad incident. It was about a year or two into my disease when one night during my sleep I awoke with that weak, shaky feeling. I could never sleep during a low blood sugar; it would always wake me up first. So in a dazed state I managed to stumble downstairs from my bedroom to the kitchen. By now I knew what I had to do, and that was to get sugar into me quickly. So in my foggy state I grabbed a glass from the cupboard to pour some orange juice. The next thing I remember was the sound of my mom screaming and trying desperately to wake me. In the worst nightmare sense of the word, I awoke to find my feet dripping with blood. Turns out that I'd gotten the glass down, and the orange juice out but then had knocked the glass onto the floor where it shattered, I then proceeded to walk all over it! Like a zombie, I walked into the front room and passed out on a chair in a low blood sugar coma.

After Mom revived me and got me to drink some orange juice, I became aware of what had transpired. The cuts weren't bad enough for stitches, and after I was fixed up and sugared up, I returned to bed. *Educational point*: The point to be made here is that a low-blood sugar coma is usually not a life threatening event because your body will eventually revive you. Your liver kicks in and starts producing sugar to compensate for the imbalance. It's the high blood sugar comas that can kill you! I relate a story of that later on.

I have watched TV shows where a person states that he almost died from a low blood sugar-induced coma! I suppose that possibly could happen, but in my experience, I always revived because I ate some candy or juice. When you eat a bunch of sweets to compensate for that low, weak feeling on top of your body's automatic "liver sugar" revival process, then your blood sugar really soars! I certainly did plenty of that over the years. Oddly I started looking forward to that low blood sugar feeling, because that meant all food and goodies were mine for the taking, and I did a good job of cleaning out the fridge from time to time! After one of those roller coaster episodes, I would have to compensate for that with more insulin.

Consuming different types of food also was a learning experience for me. I soon figured out the obvious, like anything sweet was going to ruin my blood sugar readings. As I was learning this new way to eat, certain strange effects occurred with foods that I thought were okay to eat, but had terrible effects on blood sugar. For instance, anything with corn in it, or a piece of white bread made my blood sugars soar, while a cup of ice cream had very little effect! Something about the lactic acid in milk compensated for the sugar in ice cream. I gladly remembered this fact!

By now you might begin to figure out that I wasn't the model diabetic kid. I had an unsatisfiable love of sweets; they were like a drug to me, a very bad drug that would probably end my life someday. Early on it was pounded into my head that I would someday just die from diabetes, because there was no cure. As I grew and the bad effects of the disease started to take their toll, I realized that I would die from diabetes only after I first went blind, lost the use of my legs, and lost my kidney function. Diabetes is a slow killer; it eats up your body from the inside out.

CHAPTER 5

My Loving Parents

As I reflect back, I have such warm feelings and happy memories of my parents. Mom seemed to fuss over me more than over my older siblings, because I was the baby of the family, coming along five years after my brother. I have early memories of my mother doing such loving and fun things for me like making pancakes in the shapes of animals; she could sculpt great animal art from simple Swedish pancake batter, which was very thin and runny. Today they go by the elegant name *crepes*, but we still call them flat pancakes. If my family ever eats "regular" fluffy pancakes somewhere, we leave feeling stuffed after just a few of them!

For my birthdays, I always had a very special, personalized cake and many gifts. From one year I remember a lavish Noah's Ark cake; Mom had spent the prior year collecting little plastic animals to adorn it. Mom and Dad always pulled off the grandest of holidays too; all five kids were showered with many gifts. Later in life I came across old paycheck stubs of my dad's and was shocked at how little the amount was and amazed at how they ever did it. I am sure it took them a full twelve months to pay off Christmas, just in time to do it all over again.

Contracting and living with this disease formed a special bond between my parents and me. I guess then I became their main focus of worry. Diabetes was new to them too, and educational material for it was very limited, so we all learned about it together. There were many fun activities that I wanted to do, but Mom had a way of talking me out of them. I think it was her own fear of letting me go somewhere away from of her watchful eyes, where if something were to happen, she would not be there to help me. An example is trips with our church sports young men's group. One of those trips was to California for a week with our championship softball team. It was our reward trip, and I really wanted to go, but somehow Mom convinced me that it would be hard for me to take my insulin and maintain control, so I did not attend. I respected her decisions, but I didn't always like them.

My parents did allow me to go to Scout camp four hours away in the Sawtooth Mountains. Mom had set it all up ahead of time with the camp nurse. They decided to drive me up there themselves, and when Mom and Dad had me all settled and were ready to leave, I realized for the first time how strong that bond had become. I pleaded with them not to go, and it tore my heart out to see them drive away. I rushed to my tent and cried for a half hour. One of my Scout buddies finally came around and pulled me out to go do something; after that I had a great week.

On the other side of this spectrum, there was one event that my mom really wanted me to go to, but I wanted nothing to do with it; that was Diabetes Camp—*yuck*! I could not stand the idea of going off with a bunch of other kids with the same disease and talking about it all week. I felt like I was being forced to go hang out with handicapped kids where I had the same label. I didn't want to think about diabetes, and I sure didn't want be around other damaged kids with the same disease. I won that argument; I never went. Looking back, it probably would have helped me quite a lot.

After I graduated from high school, I went away to a trade school for a year. My parents made sure that I stayed in a dorm that provided meals, so I would have adequate and regular food. My parents were two of the best; I could not have been more blessed.

I lived my life pretty much as normal, except for having to stop and pee on a stick twice a day and then take a shot of insulin. I ate pretty much what I wanted, with low sugar content of course. One thing I really grew to love was diet pop; it became my sweet reward next to ice cream. Diet pop I could drink without any guilt. Even to this day, when I don't have to worry about sugar intake, I still love the taste of diet pop and can't stand the overly sweet taste of regular pop. Now if that isn't a hypocritical taste-bud turn of events: I who couldn't seem to get enough sugar think that regular pop is too sweet! Back then there were only two kinds of diet: Fresca and Tab. I still like them both, though Tab is getting hard to find. Back then it was made with saccharin, which is a bitter-tasting sugar substitute, but I grew to like it, and I still like that bitter taste! Saccharin is found in Sweet'N Low, popularly termed "the pink stuff." I later discovered Stevia, which is all natural and comes from a plant. I like it!

CHAPTER 6

Katie: The Girl of My Dreams

I certainly must include the story of my wife, Katie as she is a big part of my success in living with diabetes. During my senior year of high school I met her; she was the girl of my dreams. I fell madly in love, and could not live without her—true statement. I guess you'd say I was completely twitter-pated!

As an adolescent I didn't have a lot of luck with girls; I thought that they all had a kind of "stuck-up cheerleader" attitude toward me. You know—"why would anyone so good-looking as us want to go out with a boy like you" attitude. Oh, I had a few dates with girls you might refer to as homely. I usually got a kiss from them after an awkward date, and then we never dated after that. When I met Katie, my whole world changed forever!

It was one late-summer night; I was driving my dad's truck around "the Cruise," as we called it. The Cruise was about a two-mile circle of connecting streets, and we

would drive around it continuously. This was a regular
activity for lonesome boys to engage in. This particular
night I just happened to be driving around alone, when I
passed a house and spotted two of the most gorgeous girls
I had ever seen sitting out on the front porch—and they
waved at me! These were beautiful blonde girls, the kind
that fill young boys' dreams. From pure shock I almost
wrecked the truck trying to stop and turn the corner
all at the same time. I had to pull over and reflect for a
moment on what had happened. This was so odd because
girls didn't wave at me, and certainly not pretty ones!
So I drove by the house again to see if I was imagining
this, and they waved again! I felt like I was having the
low-blood-sugar shakes, and weakness filled my body. I
didn't have the nerve to go back and talk to them, no way.

So I took off to my friend Stan's house, just a few blocks
away. He was a guy that had plenty of confidence talking
to girls. I screamed and pleaded with him to come with
me and talk to these girls, because I knew he would talk,
where I would just make a fool out of myself and blow
the whole opportunity. He was also very girl-hungry,
so it didn't take much convincing. We flew back to the
house, and they waved at us again, so we stopped. That
wave would be Katie's big mistake! These girls were

two sisters, Phyllis and Katie. Katie was the taller one, and I liked her right away! As I was stepping all over my tongue to say something more than an audible mumble, Stan went right into conversation with them for several minutes. There was magic that night, because I knew at that moment I could not live very long without seeing the one named Katie again.

As things turned out, we did meet again and again. When my senior year of school started, I found out that she was a sophomore and also found out where she would sit every day after lunch. I would walk back and forth in front of her for several days, stealing glances at her. Of course she started to notice this weirdo stalking her, so finally after about a solid week of this, she asked me to sit down; I was in heaven! We began dating and soon were a steady couple; I never looked back. I knew very soon that I wanted to marry her and couldn't stand the thought of not being with her. I asked her to marry me two years later, right after she graduated from high school, and today she is still my beautiful bride of thirty-three years. Incidentally, there was nothing special about why Phyllis and Katie waved at me that night because for those two sisters, they did this often, and that particular night was "truck night," or the night they waved to all trucks. I am so glad I was in a truck that night!

I could not have been more blessed with my wife, Katie, as she learned—with much patience I must add—to live with and care for me. She became the best nurse an unruly patient such as myself could ever have, and without any prior training either. Diabetes, with all of its roller coaster blood sugar levels constantly changing, went hand in hand with violent mood swings. I feel ashamed of them now, but often I could not control them. With injecting insulin three times a day, my belly and the front of my legs became very sore, so again it was Katie to the rescue, giving me shots in all my unreachable zones, but I mostly preferred them in my butt, Poor Katie! She saw my pale, deflated butt cheeks more than any woman should have to. She gets back at me often by labeling me as "Old Man Butt," meaning that I have no cheeks anymore, and keeping pants up is a new problem as I grow older. This is a problem many women would love to have, I am sure!

CHAPTER 7

My Diabetes Takes a Terrible Turn

After our second son, Alex, was born in 1988, I took a job with a major grocery store chain in Oregon. I was a meat cutter by trade, and I was unsettled on where to raise my family. So we moved everything we owned over there, but after only nine months we discovered that although vacationing on the Oregon coast was very fun, living there was totally different for us. So back to Idaho we went. It was upon our return to Idaho that my diabetes degeneration really started to show its effects. I still had a job with the same grocery company, and I began having these incredibly uncomfortable and painful attacks. I felt a burning sensation encompassing my entire body, and after about twenty minutes of that, it moved up into my head. I felt like my head was literally going to burst into flames. I thought I was taking care of myself, but as it turns out, these intense attacks were from very high blood sugars. I began to notice changes in my vision also, and as I was a meat cutter, using electric saws and sharp knives, I thought it best to have my eyes checked. I went to see a regular ophthalmologist, who immediately did not like what he saw and referred me to a specialist. This is where I was told that I was experiencing Diabetic Retinopathy, which is a weakening of the blood vessels in the eyes due to long-term fluctuating blood sugar levels. The vessels begin to leak blood into the center of the eye; if untreated, this condition would have taken my sight. For many years in early diabetes treatment, there was no way to treat this, but now there was a treatment called Pan Retinal Laser surgery.

The doctor, an ophthalmologic specialist, made it clear that I should start this laser surgery almost immediately. Due to my poor diabetes control, the blood vessels in my eyes were now rupturing and filling my eyes with blood. This surgical procedure went on for a couple of months and was the most uncomfortable thing I had ever experienced. The procedure involved sitting in the waiting area for about half an hour while the eye dilator and relaxant they put in would do its work. My eye had to be relaxed and completely dilated so that it then could be propped open. The doctor then held my eyelid open with his fingers and put his small laser gun right against my eyeball and randomly shot blasts of intense laser into the eye, sealing the ruptured blood vessels. The feeling was as if someone was poking me in the eye with every blast, and I received around three thousand blasts in each eye. This procedure could only be done on one eye at a time, and only two times a week, with about five hundred blasts per session. This was done to prevent the interior of the eye from becoming too hot and causing even worse damage. The procedure left me blind in that eye for about two hours afterward, and extremely sensitive to light. This was accompanied by the worst headache I'd ever felt.

Some of the treatments had to be done during my lunch break from work, so when I returned to cut more meat, I basically was blind in one eye while using knives and power saws! It was near the end of my treatments when one day the doctor didn't like what he saw while examining my right eye. Apparently, he had gotten the laser too hot at one point, and this created a detached retina. It was clearly his fault, and it was also one of my big mistakes, because I should have sued that doctor for malpractice. Before I knew what was happening, I was told to get to Salt Lake City immediately to see a renowned ophthalmologic surgeon, who at the time was the only doctor handling this delicate operation.

The operation was all set up for the next morning, and I left that same day. I traveled there with my dad, and then Katie followed a day later, because she was working. The procedure was a success; that doctor saved the vision in my eye, except that the images were darker and slightly bent or smeared. If I had to rely on this eye totally, I would be considered legally blind, but my good, strong left eye balanced things out, and I can function fine. There are certain things that I will never enjoy again like viewing the stars vivid and bright, as they once were; now they are a little fuzzy. Watching a 3-D movie doesn't give the same enjoyment either, because I have also lost some of my depth perception, and those 3-D images don't jump out anymore. All in all, I do quite well with the sight I have, and in the next life, when my body is restored to its perfect state, I will enjoy looking into the bright, clear heavens again.

CHAPTER 8

A New Job, a New Start

It was in the early winter of 1992, when after a period of being laid off from my present job because of a slowdown in business, I was offered a meat manager's position in Wendell, Idaho. This was the company I had been with, but only on a part-time basis. This was a great new start for my family and me. We moved from Boise where we had only been renting a house, to Jerome Idaho where we found and bought a home almost immediately. I was very busy getting the meat market running profitably again, which wasn't an easy task. There was lots of pressure on me, and along with that, getting settled in our new surroundings. Life was good though and I felt good about my job.

It hit me as a surprise one day when I started having stomach problems. I was throwing up constantly, but I thought it was only the flu. So I stayed home from work one weekend and thought I was getting better. When Monday came, I returned to work, and the stomach problems returned also. I got progressively worse and the symptoms continued. I also became very lethargic to the point that just moving was a task. I felt something had to be wrong and so I went to see my diabetes doctor. While examining me and scratching his head a bit at my symptoms, he decided to take a blood sugar test. He came back into the exam room and with a startled look he said, "Have you checked your blood sugar lately?" I realized immediately that I had not for some time. With all that was going on, I just put my diabetes on autopilot. *Educational Point*: diabetes is one disease that you can't ignore or put on autopilot!

The doctor said to me, "*Your blood sugar is 1,250!*" Normal is around 90 to 120. I had the equivalent of red molasses running through my veins! He further said, "I can't believe that you are standing here in front of me. By all medical accounts you should be in a coma!" He immediately placed me in the hospital to keep me alive. *Education Point*—when blood sugar gets that high, the body rejects insulin therapy. So they kept me in the hospital for five days and slowly added insulin back into my system until it would accept it. Yes, it was stupid of me to ignore my diabetes; as I stated earlier, I was never a model diabetic. I always hated the illness and tried to pretend it wasn't a part of my life. That little experience almost took my life, and I was knocked back into the reality of taking better care of myself.

Life continued on; my meat shop had good profit numbers, but the rest of the store did not, and it closed after two years. I could see the writing on the wall earlier so I began negotiating with the only other grocery store in that little town, and soon secured the position of meat manager there. I was employed there for only two more years, and then went to work for a chain of small markets in our home town of Jerome and the surrounding valley. It was here that carpal tunnel syndrome developed in my hands and wrists. Carpal tunnel syndrome is a condition that paralyzes the hands, due to pinched nerves in the wrist canal. It is common in meat cutters, because of repetitious cutting in cold environments. It was very painful at times and sometimes I was unable to hold a knife. I was able to get a work release and compensation to have my hands operated on. After a long session of healing and occupational testing, I was advised to stop cutting meat as my occupation. I was actually grateful for the opportunity to get out of this profession. I tried some different jobs and one of those, a delivery job with an office supply company, I did well at and opened many new accounts, but the income was low and I was feeling more and more depressed each day.

CHAPTER 9

The Accident that changed everything

In the late fall of 1997, our financial problems were causing increased tension, which didn't play well with my diabetes control. One Sunday we felt we needed a road trip as a family, so decided to drive to Craters of the Moon National Monument Park, not far from Sun Valley, and about one and a half hours from our home. We got there early in the afternoon and hiked all over the park, which has extinct volcanic rock mountains and caverns. We did a lot of climbing and hiking and really wore ourselves out! At about five o'clock we had a nice picnic dinner, which included home-bottled peaches for dessert. We were full and tired but still had the long trip home.

Katie decided to drive first, and we agreed that after a quick nap, I would finish the trip. It was about thirty minutes later that I vaguely remember waking in a half-conscious state, noticing our car on the shoulder of the road. I yelled to Katie that she was off the road, and after that, I don't remember much of anything. It turns out that Katie had fallen asleep at the wheel, veered off the road, then overcorrected and back across the other lane, and crashed our car into a huge 2 ton boulder. The force of the impact was so severe that it split this boulder right in half and flipped the car over—how many times we will never know.

As I came to a foggy consciousness, I was in an ambulance and all I could hear was my son, Alex jabbering away. I think I told him to be quiet, but didn't realize it then that if he was talking normal, he must be all right. I didn't realize exactly where I was either. Alex and I were taken to a local hospital which was over an hour away, and it was a very bumpy and painful ride. My diagnosis there was that my neck and arm were broken. Miraculously my other son, Ian, who was thrown from the car while flipping at 65 mph, suffered only a cut on his ear and his arm. Alex, who had been doing all the talking in the ambulance, only got a rash from the seat belt—because he had kept his on. Ian and I had taken our seat belts off so we could rest comfortably! Poor Katie took the major impact and ended up with a broken neck and back, a crushed pelvis and foot. She had to be extricated from the car as it was crushed around her.

She was injured so severely that they Life-Flighted her
directly to the trauma hospital in Boise; at one point she
stopped breathing and had to be resuscitated. We both
underwent many surgeries and stayed in the hospital for
several weeks. As I recovered, I learned of something
that had happened to me while at the county hospital,
something that would jump-start my eventual kidney
failure. I found out that while I was there, they had
injected me with a dye to do a CT scan. This caused my
already-failing kidneys to shut down and they had to
be restarted. I was later flown to the trauma hospital in
Boise, because the test revealed I had breaks in my neck
in four critical places, which this hospital couldn't treat
me for. We continued to recover at home and couldn't
work for the next six months. After that healing time, I
returned to my delivery job part time, but the company
soon informed me that it was their policy that I couldn't
drive for them because of my diabetes.

I decided to learn a new profession at the junior college
in my town. In the fall of 1998, I enrolled in the
Carpentry program, and along with that I took Computer
Operations, Math and English writing courses. I really
did well in all of that, except for one thing. One day
near the end of my carpentry course, the instructor was

observing a project I had sanded to a beautiful finish. He pointed out small sand marks in the finish that I could not see. Apparently my eyes were bad enough that I would never be employed as a finish carpenter. I loved to build with wood, but I knew that my career choices were limited. In the next semester, I was busy completing all my schoolwork and my final wood project was under way. It was during this time around March of 1999, that I began again to have stomach problems.

CHAPTER 10

The Worst News becomes the Best News

At first I didn't know what was up, because what I thought was the stomach flu didn't go away after a few days. I was throwing up about once a day, and I decided to go see my diabetic specialist, who had also been my regular doctor for about the last fifteen years. As I relate this part of my story, keep in mind that he had cared for me and monitored my diabetes all these years and had kept regular lab tests on me; he knew that my kidneys were diminishing in function. I continued going back to him about these stomach problems for about one month, and each time he gave me different pills to try to calm my ills. The pills were having no effect, so I would work on my wood project and run to the restroom about every hour to throw up. It was now late March, I had completed my solid maple butcher's block, and it was beautiful! I wanted so much to buy it, but I was a poor student with a family to support, and only part-time work income, so off to the student auction it went. It sold for around two hundred dollars, and I was sorry to see it go.

As April began I was busy trying to finish up my last test projects so I could finish this course and receive my technical certificate. The stomach problems got worse and the throwing up was happening about every half hour now. I was so frustrated with my doctor that I had to see someone else and get some relief. I finally went to see the college campus nurse, because it was a free clinic for students. She performed several tests, but could not determine anything definite. I told her about all the medicines I was taking. She then asked if I'd had a blood test lately. It dawned on me that with all the times I had been in to see my doctor, not once had he thought to test my blood, this same blood that was beginning to boil toward him. The nurse drew my blood and sent the test off for processing. She had to send it out because this was a small clinic with no lab. Two days later she called me and asked me to come right in. From the tone of her voice, I could tell that something seemed very bad, but what could it be? As I drove across campus, my mind was teeming with a flurry of things that could be wrong. Was it a real bad stomach ulcer or, even worse, cancer? Preparing for the worst, I entered the office. She sat me

down and with much soberness in her voice; she told me
that my kidneys had all but stopped working!

How, how can this be happening now? That thought
screamed through my head. It had been a year and a half
since that horrific accident, and I thought I was finally
fully recovered. Then my thoughts turned to rage—rage
at my so-called diabetic specialist doctor, who should
have known all these signs of kidney failure, who had all
my past test results in front of him, and who had never
once figured out that my stomach problems could be
linked to all the toxins building up in my system due to
my kidneys not cleaning the waste out anymore.

From that moment on, I never saw that doctor again.
I reported all this to the clinic where he practiced, but
of course he was a doctor of great respect, and they
protected him and dismissed my claims. After I broke
this terrible news to my mother, who was also seeing
this same doctor because she was beginning to contract
adult-onset diabetes, she also did not go to him ever
again. Through the campus nurse, I was referred to a
local Nephrologist (kidney specialist). He told me that
I needed to get started on dialysis as soon as possible. I

was set up with an appointment to go to the kidney clinic in Boise.

After I had come to terms with this news, I had to break it to my family. This was not easy, and I believe I took the news better than they did. They were all very upset. "What are you going to do?" was the most common question I heard. Through living this whole life with diabetes process I seem to have developed a greater mental strength. A lifetime of living with the perils and pains of diabetes and living through that near-fatal accident gave me the strength to calmly say, "I can deal with this too."

In Boise I met with my Nephrologist, and a very lengthy appointment ensued. He told me what had to take place to get me ready for kidney dialysis. I was given two choices. One was peritoneal dialysis, which involves surgically installing an apparatus under the skin and through the wall of the abdomen. In this method, a special cleansing fluid is pumped into the peritoneal cavity, the area between the skin wall and the stomach wall of the abdomen. The fluid then circulates with the blood there and acts as the kidneys do to cleanse the blood of toxins. The fluid is left in four hours and then has to be drained back out. This had to be done three to four times per day. The second option is called hemodialysis, which involves being hooked up to a machine at a clinic for four hours while the blood is filtered by this machine. Peritoneal dialysis is what I chose, because it lets you have more mobility, and you can actually travel away from home and do it in different places. With hemodialysis, you can't really leave town for more than one day.

One of my most noteworthy trips was when Katie and I traveled clear across the state to attend a rock concert I had won tickets to. As we traveled there I put the fluid into my system, then we attended the concert, and afterward, on the way home, I drained off the old fluid! I had a special heating box that I carried in my car; it was powered by the cigarette lighter adapter. This kept the fluid at body temperature, so when I injected it, it didn't shock my body. After a while of doing this procedure, it flowed along pretty smoothly. It took a minor surgical procedure to install the tube into my body. This special orifice opened directly into my gut now, and I had to be seriously careful about opening it. I was cautioned and trained over and over to be very careful when opening this tube.

Educational point: The inside of your body is a completely sterile environment, and you cannot allow anything to invade there, or a bad infection could take place.

While my graft was healing, I couldn't use it for the dialysis process, so I got to experience hemodialysis for two weeks. This is the closest thing to prison I have ever experienced. You must show up at this clinic every other day and be hooked up to this big blood-filtering device and sit there for four hours. By the way, this device is hooked to you by these two big tubes that go directly to your main arteries, and they become a part of you; not very much fun at all. Since my tubes were temporary, they were placed in my neck and taped down while not being used; talk about feeling like Frankenstein! After just a few of these appointments, I couldn't believe that some people with the choice for a transplant actually chose this method instead!

While I was being trained to do all of this in Boise, I was also counseled by my doctor for a kidney transplant operation. During my first workup visit to LDS Hospital in Salt Lake City, Katie and I had a very serious and life-altering conversation with my transplant surgeon. It was determined by my labs diagnosis that I would be a good candidate for a Kidney/Pancreas transplant that was to be done all at the same time. Katie and I were blown away! It was explained to us that I had two choices here. I could have a kidney only, and then, in approximately eight years, it too would be worn out by the diabetes, and I would have to go through this process again, provided I was still healthy enough for another operation. The alternative procedure, which was a no-brainer for me, was to have the kidney/pancreas transplant operation. Not only would this in all practical theory give me a new, well-functioning kidney, but the new pancreas would cure my diabetes forever, *Forever*!

The doctor concluded his orientation speech with, "This is a big decision; go home and you and your wife discuss it for a week and then call us back with your decision." In what seemed like the twinkling of an eye, I turned to Katie, and we both smiled at each other, and I nodded. She knew instantly what I was thinking and nodded back at me. I turned right around to the doctor and said, "We don't have to go home and discuss it. This is the one chance I have to get a normal life back. Let's move ahead with the kidney/pancreas process."

One other benefit to this procedure was that the waiting list was shorter. Many people wait years for a transplant, and for many it never comes. I was further told that I could not be put on the list until I had raised two-thirds of the money needed, which was probably close to $250,000. One month later, miraculously, Medicare changed its conditions for this procedure and said they were now going to cover the entire amount of the operation! I was put on the waiting list in July of 1999 and got my call to come for the operation in early August of the same year! Katie and I realized this was a miracle in progress for my family and me.

CHAPTER 11

The Big Operation

During that hot two months of waiting, I was very impatient and tried to keep myself occupied and busy. I could not work because of the dialysis procedures taking place four times a day, so I started a fund-raiser to help pay for this operation. At this point I was still being told there was no Medicare insurance to cover the operation. Couple with the fact that this operation was expected to cost between $300,000 to $400,000, both Katie and I were very nervous about how we would ever pay for this. We found out however, that people were very generous. This was a very humbling thing to be a part of. My funding account was set up at a local bank where a friend from high school was the president. As money was donated, I could observe the balance. Even though it was not nearly enough, the fund grew to over $7,500 at the time I got my call.

It was a very hot and muggy day in early August. Never knowing when "the call" would come, we were told by the transplant team to always be ready to go. Our

instructions were to have a bag packed and be ready
in an instant to leave for Salt Lake City. My transplant
coordinator was a jolly older lady that reminded me
very much of my own Aunt June. She would call me
every other week to check on me. I was out under my
old van changing the oil so it would be trip-ready, just
in case. I was feeling quite exhausted, a side effect of
the peritoneal dialysis treatments. When she called me, I
wasn't expecting anything out of the ordinary. She asked
how I was feeling, and I told her honestly that I was very
tired and worn out. Without hesitation she said, "We have
a possible match for you, how soon can you get here?"
I questioned her because I couldn't believe what I was
hearing. I think a little shock was setting in. I told her I
had to finish my oil change and then we would be on the
road, and that is exactly what we did!

It's a three-and-a-half to four-hour trip from our home
to the hospital in Salt Lake City; we made it in under
three! I didn't even take a shower after I finished with
the motor oil. We threw everything in the car, including
my younger son, and off we went like a guided missile!
My twelve-year-old son stayed at home, and his aunt
from Boise came down the next morning to pick him
up. I don't remember much about the trip, as we were

"flying low" and it was dark soon after we left. We had been counseled that we might have to make several trips like this one, because a perfect organ match could not be determined until final tests were performed at the hospital on the harvested organs. Usually these organs were coming from accident victims, and they had to be deemed "in good condition" to be used. We arrived around 10:15 p.m. at the hospital. After a stressful hour's wait, we were shocked to hear that the organs were healthy and were a perfect match; the operation was on!

After all my registration was in place, I was escorted to a preparation room, where I was thoroughly and embarrassingly washed from head to toe by a female nurse. Then it was time to be cleaned on the inside—yes, I said the inside! Since I had no time to fast and evacuate my system, a series of enemas was prescribed and performed. Sorry to be graphic here, but having a gallon of water pumped up your butt and then being asked to hold it as long as possible is an impossible task I can assure you! This was performed, I think four times. I lay in the bed there with Katie by my side for another agonizing three hours. Alex had fallen asleep in a special waiting area where he was bedded down for the night. Katie stayed with me as long as she could. We talked about our lives and tried not to think about bad things that might happen. Finally at three in the morning they came for me. I hugged Katie very tightly and told her how much I loved her; then she joined Alex in the waiting area. She told me later that she hadn't slept much.

They placed me on a gurney and wheeled me out into the cold hallway with only a thin hospital gown covering me. As we traveled through various corridors, it became even colder. This is where I first experienced and fell in love with heated blankets. They covered me with one, and it felt so good and comforting that after this big surgery, whenever I had another surgery, of which there would be many, I couldn't wait to ask for these extremely hot blankets! I lay there on the gurney just outside of my operating room for what seemed like an eternity; in reality it was another forty-five minutes. Now it had really settled in what was about to take place, and I started to shake even more. Then a most bizarre and curious thing happened, which I shall never forget. All of a sudden, the Transport Assistant came hurriedly down the hall pulling a small ice cooler on wheels. I knew in an instant that there were my new organs. As he went into the operating room, he was followed by several nurses, assistants, and doctors, among whom, of course, was Dr.

Belknap, the chief transplant surgeon. I was wheeled in right behind them. From my years working as a butcher, I recognized the coldness of the operating room; because it felt just like a meat locker, very cold and dry. They scooted me over onto this metal slab that I'm sure was pre-refrigerated! I made a desperate plea for a hot blanket as I started to shiver uncontrollably. I think this was in part adrenaline coursing through my system. There were a few words of comfort offered, and then the anesthetist told me I was now going to go to sleep.

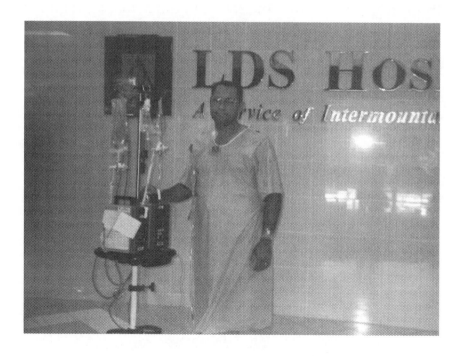

I came to consciousness slowly and calmly, an
experience I still love. It is like the best sleeping-in-late
you can experience, with no reason to really wake up. I
was surrounded by my son, Katie, my parents and parents
in-law as I recall. They were there with smiles and happy
greetings. After I spent a couple of hours coming around,
in came the nurse, and to my utter shock she said, "It's
time to get up, the doctor wants you on your feet!" By
this time I had started to feel some discomfort from my
incision site, and from what I could imagine, I was cut
from sternum to penis! In reality, my incision was about
eight inches and started at the base of my pelvic area.
Well, as instructed, I first rolled onto my side and tried to
pull myself upright. It didn't happen. As I made a second
attempt with the nurse's help, I dragged myself upright
on the bed. The pain screamed through my gut like I
had just been slashed with a sword; that was step one.
Step two was standing. The pain hadn't subsided, and
I pulled myself onto my legs. Wobbly and weak, it felt
unexpectedly good to be standing. I walked to the end of
the bed, turned around, and came back. I sat back down
and as I lay back down, that searing pain returned. That
was my first of many such therapy sessions.

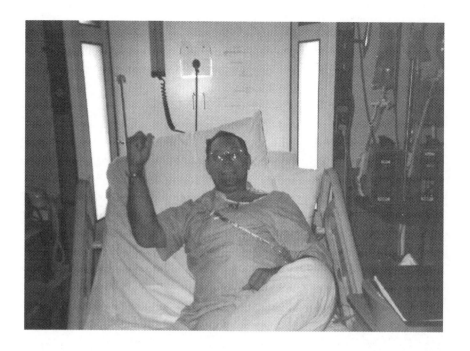

CHAPTER 12

A Famous Tornado and a Recovery

Now for a bit of strange Utah history. After one full
day of recovery, I rose from my bed again with that
all-too-familiar gut pain and decided to take my first
walk out of my room. I had with me two rolling stands
with three bottles each hanging off of them along with a
couple of monitoring devices. I don't know what all this
fluid was they were giving me, but as I recovered, it was
a personal victory each time a bottle was removed. With
Katie supporting me, we went out into the hall to a large
picture window looking over the Salt Lake valley. As
we took in the view, we began to feel the pressure of the
wind against the glass as it got stronger and stronger. All
of a sudden we couldn't believe our eyes, as a large black
funnel cloud flew by the window, within it the entire roof
of a house! This was *Wizard of Oz* stuff for sure. We later
found out that we were smack dab in the middle of, what
is now called the famous Utah tornado of 1999. This
freak storm tore down several buildings in its path and
killed one person.

It quickly moved up the hill above Salt Lake City, where it wrapped itself around the LDS Hospital, tore up several homes next to it, and sheared off all the hospital's trees at ground level! Even odder, it turned out the roof that we saw blow by my window was the same roof that had been on the guest house where Katie and my youngest son were staying during my surgery. Strangely enough, their luggage was untouched. This now-famous tornado did a lot of damage, and the recovery effort involved a great number of Utah residents. It was thus named "The Spirit of Recovery." Two years later, I became involved in an organ transplant support group and I used that same slogan to promote our cause, coupling it with a classic car show for transplant survivors. The Spirit of Recovery Cruisin' Car Show and luau picnic—very fun and memorable times.

Back to my own recovery, I had to take a mountain of pills at first, and I do mean a mountain. I should mention also that during this whole ordeal my stomach was very upset, to the point of throwing up constantly, and food didn't taste right. I think it had something to do with the surgery in my abdomen. All these new pills were taking a toll on my system, and there were so many in the beginning that the pharmacist gave me a notebook to keep track, containing several pages of each pill's breakdown. I had several visits from the pharmacist too; he educated me on what each pill was for. It was all about learning a whole new lifestyle, but I was not complaining; this new lifestyle was 100 percent better than my old one. A new life without diabetes, without three injections per day, without the mood swings, and without those head-burning-up feelings, without the bottoming-out feelings of low blood sugar and then, the rebounding high blood sugars.

I stayed in the hospital recovery floor for fourteen restless days; sleeping in a hospital bed I found to be next to impossible. Trying to drift off was usually disturbed by constant tests throughout the night. I would finally fall asleep at four in the morning, and then at seven it was time to wake up and prepare for breakfast! I feel sure those nurses were against patients getting a good night's sleep. Most of the food was inedible in my opinion. I had a lot of trouble just swallowing it. Toward the end of my stay, I was told that I could order *real* food from the café/coffee shop downstairs—a fact that they had somehow left out! I immediately started having corn dogs and hamburgers and milkshakes sent up—yes, milkshakes without any side effects. I loved it!

The day finally came when it was time to leave, and believe it or not, I didn't want to go! I was very apprehensive about it. I felt unsure that I could care for myself on my own, and begged the doctor to let me stay a few more nights. This wasn't anything he hadn't heard before from transplant patients. He calmly looked at me and said, "A hospital is for sick people, you are in good health again, and you need to get away from all these sick people." He was right, of course; I couldn't disagree with that logic. I left the hospital for what I hoped was the last time.

CHAPTER 13

Outpatient Recovery

My recovery also required me to stay close to the hospital for two weeks. I stayed with the parents of a good friend from my teen years. His mother, Ruth, took great care of me, and his father, Glenn ran me to and from the hospital whenever I needed tests. Since I spent a lot of time at my friend's house in high school, I felt very comfortable staying with them; they were like second parents to me. One pill I was taking severely depleted my immune system and outside of the hospital I was in danger of picking up any viral sickness. My instructions for the next two months were to avoid public gatherings and children in general. At first I slept a lot, which felt great, because I was once again in a real bed. Ruth fed me good stuff like oatmeal for breakfast, and for lunch, sandwiches with homemade bread, I was in heaven! I took long walks to build up my strength, and felt good that I could go a bit farther each day. One day near the end of my stay, I decided to venture out and walked to the theater that was three blocks away to see the newest movie release. It was *The Sixth Sense*, a very creepy movie that I loved until I had to walk home alone, and this was in south Salt Lake City, not the best of neighborhoods to be walking at twilight. I didn't sleep very well that night either, and I had to leave the light on because in the movie, there were several scenes of dead people walking around! My bedroom was way in the back of this old house, and I kept a close eye on the lit hallway all night long. In my imagination, I was sure a dead person was going to stroll by my bedroom door at any time!

CHAPTER 14

Dr. Belknap

My excellent surgeon through this whole experience
was Doctor LeGrand Belknap. From what I was to
discover later, he was the head surgeon of the LDS
transplant team, and for one good reason: he was the
best. Although he had a very strange bedside manner, he
was the one you wanted performing an operation of this
magnitude. He worked long hours, mostly late into the
night and early mornings. There were a couple of times
while in my hospital bed I would wake from sleep to
see him standing over me just watching me. There was
one night I couldn't sleep so I was watching TV at two
a.m. He strolled into my room and asked me what I was
watching and then he proceeded to sit down and watch
with me for about a half hour. Without saying much
of anything, he then got up and walked out! He never
had much of anything to say to me. He wasn't married,
mostly because I am sure he didn't have time for a wife!
Transplant surgery was his life. The nurses liked to tell
me stories of this odd doctor. One story that really stuck

with me was when he had a date set with a certain lady one night. Well there is no set schedule for transplant surgery; when the organs become available, they have to be put in soon after. He had a late-night surgery but didn't cancel his date. Instead he had a nurse call this lady and tell her that he would still be by for their date, but that it would be about three a.m.! He took each surgery very personally, and if there was a problem, he was going to address it right there at LDS.

CHAPTER 15

To and From the Hospital I Go

After I returned home to Jerome, there were four different incidents that would require my return to the hospital in Salt Lake City. As stated, Dr. Belknap took no chances with transplanted organs, and if there was any possibility of losing my organs, Dr. Belknap wanted me back in Salt Lake City immediately! The first time I was flown back by an airplane ambulance and twice by regular ground ambulance; the fourth time we drove ourselves. The three emergency trips I will always remember. Two hours on a small plane where all I could do was lie on a bed and stare at the ceiling, which was about six inches away from my face was very unpleasant. All these emergency trips were at Dr. Belknap's insistent request!

The first and most memorable return was about two weeks after I had gone back to Idaho. One morning when I was struggling to take my mountain of pills, I got one stuck in my throat and choked. The exertion of coughing it up caused my long abdominal incision to open like a zipper! It was a very eerie feeling, and I could feel the internal juices running down my leg. At first I didn't believe anything had happened except that I had wet my pants. I think I was in shock when I saw the open wound with body stuff hanging out! I didn't jump up yelling and screaming, and surprisingly, it didn't hurt either. Katie was about to leave for work, and I calmly told her what had just occurred. Well she went into an all-out panic, and I thought she was going to pass out; then we would both have to be checked into the hospital! After Katie had calmed down, she drove me to the hospital, and a good surgeon and friend of ours from church carefully checked me over and then called Dr. Belknap.

He, of course was not taking any chances with my organs being lost, so the surgeon in Jerome set up an emergency flight and I was rushed by airplane ambulance to Salt Lake City. After a major cleaning of my abdominal cavity, an extensive reconstructive sew-up took place. I had to be sewn up on the inside abdominal wall and the outer skin had to be left open. This was very gross to look at, with a gaping two-inch-wide gash running down my middle for about five inches. What the doctors told me next, I really had to see to believe. They said this big hole would start to close on its own like a zipper closing from the bottom up!

Over the next two months, amazingly, it did just that. Since these were non-dissolving stitches inside this opening, they had to come out before this big hole could heal. I was very concerned when the stitches began to disappear from my sight with the healing taking place, and I started calling the doctor every week. Finally, near the end of the second month, Katie and I drove back down to Salt Lake City to the hospital for outpatient surgery to remove the stitches. During this process, there were two tubes crossing inside my abdomen for drainage. These also had to be pulled out. As the first one was pulled out, it felt like someone had just dragged a jagged knife across my gut! It was every bit as painful as the first time I had to stand after surgery, but all ended well with the assistance of pain medication.

CHAPTER 16

Back to Salt Lake—
Merry Christmas!

After returning home, I began to fully heal and my
life was returning to normal. I just had one regiment
to keep each day, just as with my insulin injections
from the past, I now had to make sure I took my main
anti—rejection pills twice daily; it was a good trade-off.
As recovery progressed, my labs indicated that I could
decrease the number of pills I was taking. One pill they
had me on was Prednisone. It is a common steroid used
for anti-rejection, but it has one especially undesirable
feature; most people that were put on it couldn't get off
of it. The side effects were severe also: hair falling out,
distorted facial features, and bone density loss. When the
doctor told me not many people were successful dropping
that drug, I said to him, "Just try me, because I will
get off of it." So he started to lower the dose by a half
milligram each week for about eight weeks, until I was
down to just half a milligram. I then stopped it altogether.

I believe that I used mind over matter on that one, and it worked.

Having a loss of bone density caused an incident. While visiting some family on Christmas Eve, I slipped on some ice and simply fell down, but my leg got caught up under me and snapped like a twig. After a very depressing night in the local hospital, I was told that my leg had a compound fracture and had to be surgically pinned with a steel rod placed permanently in my leg bone. That took place the next day on Christmas, and under the direct advice from Dr. Belknap, they monitored my vitals for the next two days. At the end of day three, I started to develop a low-grade fever that could not be lowered. When Dr. Belknap heard of this, the local hospital was instructed to get me to Salt Lake again as soon as possible. That turned into another long ambulance ride back to LDS Hospital. After two long weeks to clear an infection and bring the fever down, I was given a clean bill of health and returned to Idaho.

CHAPTER 17

Salt Lake City—One More Time

The third trip back was a bit more serious. Several months had passed, and it was early spring in the year 2000. Katie and I made a short trip to Boise for the day. We were craving seafood, and a friend suggested this new place that was touted as being very good. It *was* good, except for one thing. We would discover later that the restaurant made fresh tartar sauce with mayonnaise but failed to refrigerate it on the serving table. After returning home that night, I became violently ill. It was so bad that I became delirious and eventually passed out while attempting to get to the bathroom. I remember nothing of this whole ordeal, but it turned into a night of terror for Katie and my sons. They tried to lift me but were unable. They then called 911 and an ambulance came with instructions to take me directly to LDS Hospital. Most people would have just got a little sick from eating bad tartar sauce, but for someone with a zero immune system, it was almost deadly. My poor wife and boys suffered for three days while I lay unconscious in the intensive care unit. When I finally came to, the nurse said they weren't sure I was going make it. Several more days passed to get me stable, and then it was time to return home again.

CHAPTER 18

A Full Recovery

One and a half years passed without any more incidents, but I still felt a need to be close to LDS Hospital. I felt it would be good just in case something traumatic were to happen again. We set in motion plans to look for work down there and move when we could. I planned a little time to look at the job scene in Salt Lake City while my family and I were on a trip to Las Vegas to see a NASCAR race. As we pulled into the downtown area, I spotted a sign on a new luxury hotel that was being built for the 2002 Winter Olympics. It read, now hiring for all positions. I had decided earlier to take my hand doctor's advice and give up on meat cutting, and since I had some limited building maintenance experience from the first job after my transplant, I decided to apply. I had left this first job because I still wasn't 100 percent recovered and got exhausted easily.

I filled out the application, and they interviewed me right on the spot for a mechanical maintenance position and then hired me that day! I couldn't believe it! The hotel supervisors wanted me to start the next week, but I told them I had to move down from Idaho and needed a little time. I started my new job three weeks later and moved just myself to Salt Lake City for the time being. I found out later that not many people had applied for the mechanical maintenance positions, and they needed people soon!

I enjoyed my new job and since I had no family with me presently, I spent my free time with my transplant social worker from the hospital helping him with the support group there. I had a good time doing that. One day he asked me if I would like to help by talking to other people going through or considering an organ transplant. I found that I enjoyed it immensely, and it gave me great satisfaction to give something back. I received many compliments for my services, mostly from patients in the hospital. It seemed to give them renewed hope to see someone who made it through to good health again. I could certainly relate because when I was in the hospital clinging to life, sometimes I felt like I would never get out! Working with the support group was a lot of fun; my social worker was Hawaiian, so he knew how to throw good luau picnics, and one time he asked me to put on the aforementioned classic car show. It was for transplant recipients and donors who liked to show off their car projects. I had one of my own, so it was double fun for me to show off my classic 1966 Ford pickup. I still have it today.

CHAPTER 19

Life Continues

The rest of my story is history in the making, I guess. I am going on my thirteenth year with my new organs, and they are still functioning fine. In fact, my kidney function tests have shown steady improvement. I have my Savior Jesus Christ to thank for that. I guess some may ask if all these problems I went through were really worth it. Let me just say, I would do it all over again in a heartbeat! Juvenile diabetes is no way to live, and is a life filled with medical hazards. The way I feel now is normal, and it took me a long time to understand how normal really feels, but I can tell you now, *normal feels great*!

On a final note, I want to stick my tongue out at all the life insurance companies that turned me down for coverage because I was just too big of a risk, and they all felt certain I would drop dead at any moment. To all those underwriting nurses that turned their noses up at me and said to me bluntly and laughingly over the phone, "Sir, there is no cure for diabetes" I retaliated their snooty jeers smugly, but quietly with "why yes there is, I've got one, it's called a t-r-a-n-s-p-l-a-n-t—ever heard of that?" That always seemed to shut them up.

Finally, my mother who passed away at eighty-five, and to whom I dedicate this story because of the great care and attention she gave me all those years with my terrible disease. I know it aged her and my father significantly, but like a mother, she would have done it all over again for any of her children. So for her I end my story with its title, repeating what the doctors confirmed to her all those years ago, "Yes Virginia, there is a cure for diabetes."

ABOUT THE AUTHOR

The author is presently fifty-three years old, and he tells a story of how he lived his life fighting the debilitating disease of juvenile diabetes, his unique slant on his cure and how it changed his life. This is his first book.

Printed in the United States
By Bookmasters